U.S.A. TRAVEL GUIDES

SOUTH DAKOTA

BY ANN HEINRICHS • ILLUSTRATED BY MATT KANIA

The Child's World®
childsworld.com

Published by The Child's World®
1980 Lookout Drive • Mankato, MN 56003-1705
800-599-READ • www.childsworld.com

Photo Credits
Photographs ©: Shutterstock Images, cover, 1, 37 (top),
37 (bottom); National Park Service, 7, 28; Centrill Media/
Shutterstock Images, 8; Ioppear CC2.0, 11; Rich Koele/
Shutterstock Images, 12; Benjamin Brayfield/Rapid
City Journal/AP Images, 15; Danae Abreu/Shutterstock
Images, 16; Nagel Photography/Shutterstock Images,
19, 31; Becky Tycz/Tyndall Tribune & Register, 20; Loren
Kerns CC2.0, 23; J.Q. Miller/Library of Congress, 24;
Joseph Sohm/Shutterstock Images, 27; Chet Brokaw/
AP Images, 32; iStockphoto, 35

ISBN 9781503819818
LCCN 2016961625

Printing
Printed in the United States of America
PA02334

Ann Heinrichs is the author
of more than 100 books
for children and young
adults. She has also enjoyed
successful careers as a
children's book editor and
an advertising copywriter.
Ann grew up in Fort Smith,
Arkansas, and lives in
Chicago, Illinois.

About the Author
Ann Heinrichs

Matt Kania loves maps and, as a
kid, dreamed of making them. In
school he studied geography and
cartography, and today he makes
maps for a living. Matt's favorite
thing about drawing maps is
learning about the places they
represent. Many of the maps
he has created can be found in
books, magazines, videos, Web
sites, and public places.

About the
Map Illustrator
Matt Kania

*On the cover: You'll find many colorful rock
formations at Badlands National Park.*

OUR SOUTH DAKOTA TRIP

SOUTH DAKOTA

Hey—let's take a tour of South Dakota! You'll find it's a great place to explore.

You'll walk the streets of Wild West towns. You'll watch herds of buffalo galloping by. You'll see giant faces carved in mountainsides. You'll visit a palace covered with corn. You'll roam through **prairies** and see **missile** sites. And you'll hang out with real cowboys!

Are you ready for adventure? Then settle in and buckle up. It's time to hit the road!

WELCOME TO
SOUTH
DAKOTA

Have you seen these faces before? They're four U.S. presidents. And they're carved right into the mountain. You're visiting Mount Rushmore!

This awesome mountain is in the Black Hills. Among these hills are forests, canyons, and caves. The Badlands are southeast of the Black Hills. This is a dry region with strangely shaped rocks.

The Missouri River is South Dakota's major river. It flows south, then southeast, through the state. To the west are rugged canyons and rolling plains. Eastern South Dakota has rich farmland. It's dotted with many small lakes, too.

Mount Rushmore honors four famous presidents.

THE BUFFALO ROUNDUP AT CUSTER STATE PARK

Cowboys and cowgirls gallop across the plains. They're herding buffalo into **corrals**. It's the Buffalo Roundup at Custer State Park!

About 1,300 buffalo roam through this park. Every year they're rounded up. They get medical care, and some are sold.

This park is near Custer in the Black Hills. Many other animals make their homes here. Some live high in the mountains. You'll see mountain goats and bighorn sheep in this area. On the prairies are deer and pronghorn antelope. Prairie dogs dig tunnels to build their towns. You'll spot elk, coyotes, and wild turkeys, too.

Yeehaw! Don't miss the Buffalo Roundup at Custer State Park!

STATE TREE
BLACK HILLS SPRUCE

STATE BIRD
CHINESE RING-NECKED PHEASANT

STATE FLOWER
PASQUE

NORTH DAKOTA

MONTANA

MINNESOTA

WYOMING

Let's take the Wildlife Loop Road! That's where they're bringing all the buffalo.

Black Hills Reptile Gardens is in Rapid City. It holds the world's largest reptile collection.

Black Hills

Rapid City

Custer

Custer State Park

IOWA

NEBRASKA

Custer State Park hosts the Buffalo Wallow Chili Cook-off every year. Everyone's chili must contain buffalo meat!

The National Park Service has seven sites in South Dakota.

Lemmon's Petrified Wood Park is the world's largest petrified wood park.

NORTH DAKOTA

MONTANA

MINNESOTA

• Lemmon

Cool! The castle structure is made up of petrified wood, dinosaur bones, and mammoth bones!

• Faith

Piedmont is home to the Petrified Forest of the Black Hills.

WYOMING

• Piedmont

Black Hills

• Rapid City

Badlands

• Kadoka

The Badlands Petrified Gardens are in Kadoka.

NEBRASKA

IOWA

Dinosaurs lived in South Dakota approximately 150 million to 66 million years ago.

A dinosaur named Sue is the world's largest *Tyrannosaurus rex* skeleton. It's named after Sue Hendrickson, who found the dinosaur near the town of Faith. The skeleton is now in the Field Museum of Natural History in Chicago, Illinois.

The Museum of Geology is at the South Dakota School of Mines and Technology in Rapid City. It displays hundreds of rocks and **fossils**.

LEMMON'S PETRIFIED WOOD PARK

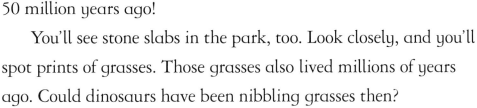

Stroll down the winding paths. This is no ordinary park. Tall, pointy structures rise from the ground. One structure even looks like a castle! Here and there are weird stumps and logs. You're wandering through the Petrified Wood Park in Lemmon.

Most things in this park are wood. But it's petrified, or turned to stone. The wood once belonged to giant trees. They were alive approximately 50 million years ago!

You'll see stone slabs in the park, too. Look closely, and you'll spot prints of grasses. Those grasses also lived millions of years ago. Could dinosaurs have been nibbling grasses then?

Those rocks were trees 50 million years ago! Check out the Petrified Wood Park.

THE MAMMOTHS OF HOT SPRINGS

Walk through the dig site. Around every corner are big bones. Some are skulls with huge, curved tusks. This is not just a big museum. It's a mammoth museum!

You're visiting the Mammoth Site Museum in Hot Springs. It's built right on a scientists' digging place. They discovered lots of mammoth bones here.

Mammoths lived here about 26,000 years ago. These massive, shaggy beasts were related to elephants. We sometimes use the word *mammoth* to mean "gigantic."

Many other animals were found in this spot, too. But mammoths were the most mammoth of them all!

Want to learn about prehistoric animals? Tour the Mammoth Site Museum!

The Mammoth Site Museum is the world's largest center for mammoth studies.

Yikes! Mammoths' teeth were the size of shoeboxes. Those teeth chomped up hundreds of pounds of plants every day!

The Museum at Black Hills Institute is in Hill City. Its exhibits include fossils, minerals, and models of dinosaurs.

• Hill City

• Hot Springs

The animals found at Hot Springs had waded into a pond. But they couldn't get out. It was too deep, and the banks were too steep. So they died there.

During the summer, kids can dig up models of bones in Hot Springs.

Two kinds of mammoths were found at Hot Springs. They are the Columbian mammoth and the woolly mammoth.

MONTANA

WYOMING

NORTH DAKOTA

MINNESOTA

NEBRASKA

IOWA

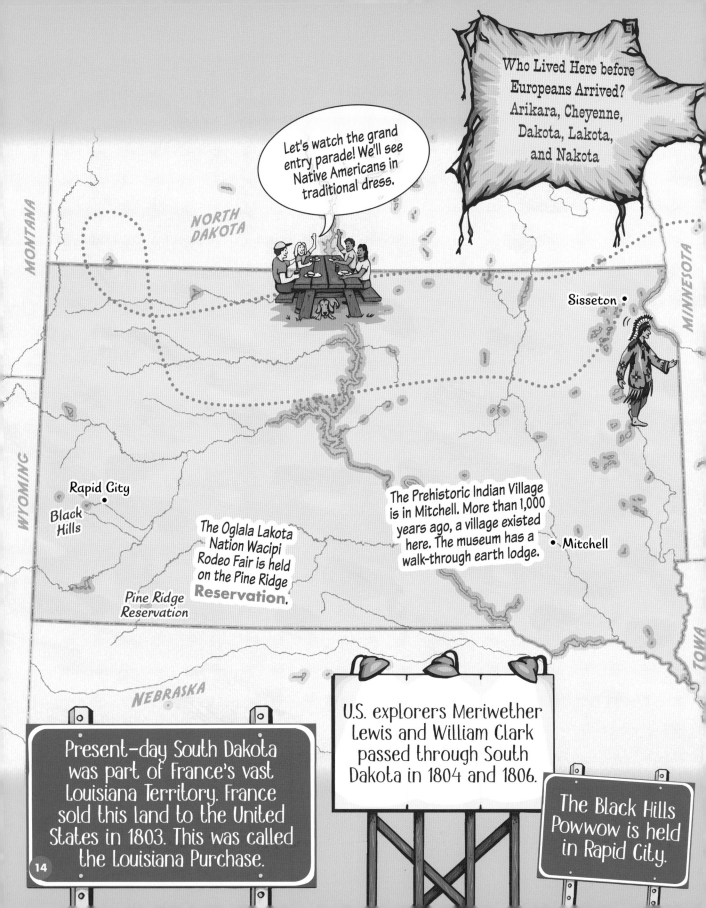

Who Lived Here before Europeans Arrived? Arikara, Cheyenne, Dakota, Lakota, and Nakota

Let's watch the grand entry parade! We'll see Native Americans in traditional dress.

MONTANA

NORTH DAKOTA

MINNESOTA

Sisseton •

WYOMING

Rapid City •

Black Hills

The Oglala Lakota Nation Wacipi Rodeo Fair is held on the Pine Ridge **Reservation.**

Pine Ridge Reservation

The Prehistoric Indian Village is in Mitchell. More than 1,000 years ago, a village existed here. The museum has a walk-through earth lodge.

• Mitchell

IOWA

NEBRASKA

Present-day South Dakota was part of France's vast Louisiana Territory. France sold this land to the United States in 1803. This was called the Louisiana Purchase.

U.S. explorers Meriwether Lewis and William Clark passed through South Dakota in 1804 and 1806.

The Black Hills Powwow is held in Rapid City.

THE SISSETON-WAHPETON OYATE WACIPI!

Watch the dancers and hear **traditional** songs. Meet the Dakota people and sample their food. It's the Sisseton-Wahpeton Oyate Wacipi! (*Wacipi* is the Dakota word for "dance" or "powwow.") It's held in Agency Village, south of Sisseton.

More than 70,000 Native Americans live in South Dakota today. Many belong to the Dakota, Lakota, or Nakota tribes. These tribes are part of the Great Sioux Nation. Their ancestors migrated from present-day Minnesota in the 1700s. The Black Hills were sacred grounds for them. This land remains sacred to Dakota, Lakota, and Nakota people today.

Native Americans perform a traditional dance at an indoor powwow in Rapid City.

THE CRAZY HORSE MEMORIAL NEAR CUSTER

Don't miss the Crazy Horse Memorial. It's a massive carving in a mountain near Custer. Only Crazy Horse's face and part of his arm have been carved so far.

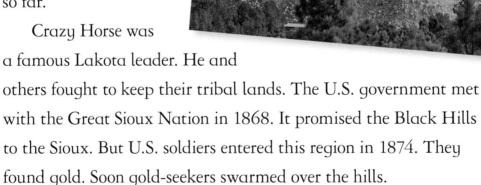

Crazy Horse was a famous Lakota leader. He and others fought to keep their tribal lands. The U.S. government met with the Great Sioux Nation in 1868. It promised the Black Hills to the Sioux. But U.S. soldiers entered this region in 1874. They found gold. Soon gold-seekers swarmed over the hills.

Crazy Horse and Dakota chief Sitting Bull fought bravely to keep their lands. But they were defeated in 1877. Later, soldiers attacked the Lakota near Wounded Knee Creek. They killed almost 300 Lakota men, women, and children.

The Crazy Horse Memorial isn't finished yet. But check it out anyway—it's still pretty amazing!

When completed, the Crazy Horse Memorial will be the world's largest mountain sculpture.

The 1868 Treaty of Fort Laramie promised that the Sioux would be able to keep their tribal lands in the Black Hills.

Let's check out the museum's cultural center. We'll find Native American art and artifacts.

The Indian Museum of North America is part of the Crazy Horse Memorial.

Crazy Horse led the Lakota in the Battle of the Little Bighorn in Montana in 1876. The Lakota, Cheyenne, and Arapaho defeated U.S. Army officer George Custer and his troops.

The massacre at Wounded Knee took place on December 29, 1890. The battle site is on today's Pine Ridge Reservation. The Wounded Knee Museum is in Wall.

Lakota chief Red Cloud led a series of battles in the 1860s to keep the U.S. government from building a road through Lakota, Cheyenne, and Arapaho hunting grounds. These conflicts are known as Red Cloud's War.

MONTANA

NORTH DAKOTA

MINNESOTA

WYOMING

Black Hills

Custer

Wall

Pine Ridge Reservation

NEBRASKA

IOWA

Let's tour the Broken Boot Gold Mine! Let's visit Mount Moriah Cemetery!

NORTH DAKOTA

MONTANA

MINNESOTA

WYOMING

Deadwood

Lead

Lead is home to the Black Hills Mining Museum and the Homestake Gold Mine.

Black Hills

Custer

IOWA

Wild Bill Hickok's real name was James Butler Hickok. He was an army scout, lawman, and gambler. He was shot and killed in Deadwood's Saloon No. 10.

Yankton

The Dakota Territorial Museum is in Yankton.

NEBRASKA

Martha Jane Canary's nickname was Calamity Jane. She was an expert at horseback riding and shooting. She usually wore men's clothes.

Dakota Territory was created in 1861. It included present-day North and South Dakota. It also included parts of Montana and Wyoming.

DEADWOOD AND THE BLACK HILLS GOLD RUSH

Have you heard of Wild Bill Hickok? How about Calamity Jane? They were colorful figures in the Wild West. Visit Deadwood, and you'll learn all about them. They once lived in this wild, lawless town. And they're both buried in Deadwood's cemetery.

Gold was discovered in this area in 1876. Thousands of miners rushed in. Deadwood, Custer, and Lead sprang up almost overnight. These mining towns were rough and rowdy.

In Deadwood, you'll see what life was like then. You'll visit the saloon and other old buildings. You can even tour an old gold mine!

Learn about life in an 1800s mining town when you visit historic Deadwood.

TABOR'S CZECH DAYS

Watch the folk dancers in their bright costumes. While you watch, munch on a *kolache*. It's a bun-shaped pastry with yummy filling inside. You're enjoying Czech Days in Tabor!

Czech **immigrants** began settling here in the 1860s. Their homeland was in eastern Europe. That area is now the Czech Republic and Slovakia. Tabor's Czechs love to celebrate their culture!

Many other immigrant groups settled in South Dakota. Some came from Germany, Norway, Russia, or Ireland. During the gold rush, many got mining jobs. Others worked hard to set up farms. They started new lives in this new land.

Learn about Czech customs and traditions at Tabor's Czech Days.

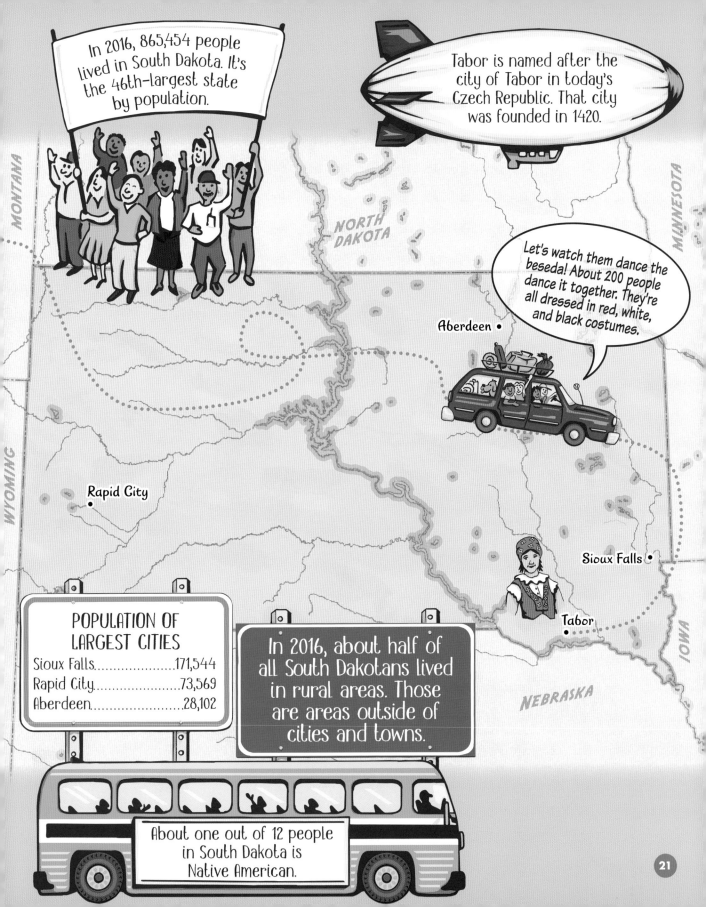

In 2016, 865,454 people lived in South Dakota. It's the 46th-largest state by population.

Tabor is named after the city of Tabor in today's Czech Republic. That city was founded in 1420.

Let's watch them dance the beseda! About 200 people dance it together. They're all dressed in red, white, and black costumes.

POPULATION OF LARGEST CITIES
Sioux Falls	171,544
Rapid City	73,569
Aberdeen	28,102

In 2016, about half of all South Dakotans lived in rural areas. Those are areas outside of cities and towns.

About one out of 12 people in South Dakota is Native American.

Let's check out the schoolhouse! We'll put on straw hats and bonnets, just like kids used to wear in the 1800s.

• De Smet

The Laura Ingalls Wilder Pageant is held in De Smet every summer.

Wilder Books Set in De Smet
By the Shores of Silver Lake
The First Four Years
Little Town on the Prairie
The Long Winter
These Happy Golden Years

Laura Ingalls taught school in De Smet. She married Almanzo Wilder there, too.

Laura Ingalls Wilder was born in Wisconsin in 1867. She was 12 when her family moved to De Smet. She died in 1957.

MONTANA

NORTH DAKOTA

MINNESOTA

WYOMING

IOWA

NEBRASKA

Have you read any books by Laura Ingalls Wilder? She wrote stories called the Little House books. Her best-known book is *Little House on the Prairie*.

Laura lived in De Smet as a girl. Several of her books take place there. One is called *Little Town on the Prairie*. And the little town is De Smet!

You can visit a farmhouse just like Laura's. It's called the Ingalls Homestead now. You can ride a horse-drawn wagon there, too. Or explore the grassy prairie. That's where Laura used to play. Imagine living there in about 1880. It would have been a great adventure!

You can ride in a covered wagon when you visit the Ingalls Homestead in De Smet.

Old-time tractors are puffing out steam. Old farm machines are plowing away. Some are pulled by sturdy horses. It's the Prairie Village Steam **Threshing** Jamboree in Madison!

Prairie Village is like a prairie town from about 1900. It shows how South Dakota's farmers lived then.

Gold brought many people to South Dakota. But thousands of others came to farm. They grew crops and raised cattle and other animals. Steam-powered farm machines made their work easier.

By the 1880s, railroads crossed the territory. Towns sprang up along the train routes. They were trade centers for farmers and ranchers.

Wow! South Dakota farmers worked hard in the early 1900s.

South Dakota was the 40th state to enter the Union. It joined on November 2, 1889.

The first public libraries in South Dakota opened in the 1880s.

Let's ride the old steam train through the village! We'll see farmhouses, schools, and shops. Then let's ride the steam-powered merry-go-round!

Madison

North Dakota and South Dakota became states on the same day. They were the 39th and 40th states to join the Union. North Dakota was 39th because it came before South Dakota in the alphabet.

Almost 584,000 people lived in South Dakota in 1910.

MONTANA

WYOMING

NORTH DAKOTA

MINNESOTA

IOWA

NEBRASKA

South Dakota's state motto is "Under God, the People Rule."

Hubert Humphrey was born in Wallace. He was vice president under President Lyndon Johnson (1965-1969).

Wow! It cost less than $1 million to build the capitol in 1910. It would cost millions more dollars to build it today!

How many people does each state send to the U.S. House of Representatives? It depends on the state's population. South Dakota has one member there. But each state sends two members to the U.S. Senate.

Yankton was the capital of Dakota Territory from 1861 to 1883. Then the territory's capital moved to Bismarck, North Dakota.

You can learn all about South Dakota history at the Cultural Heritage Center in Pierre. The center is built right into a hillside!

THE STATE CAPITOL IN PIERRE

South Dakota once had a tiny capitol. It was just a little wooden building. Inside were state government offices. In 1910, those offices got a brand-new home. It's the magnificent capitol we see today in Pierre!

South Dakota's government has three branches. One branch makes the state's laws. Its members meet in the capitol. Another branch sees that laws are carried out. The governor is the head of this branch. Judges make up the third branch. They hear cases in courts. Then they decide whether laws have been broken.

South Dakota lawmakers are hard at work inside the capitol.

First, you visit the control center. You see walls of switches and equipment. Then you visit the launch site. A huge missile once stood ready for launch there. You're touring the Minuteman missile site near Philip!

This site was one of many built in the 1960s. The missiles were weapons for the Cold War. This war developed after World War II (1939–1945). The United States was on one side. And the Soviet Union was on the other. No war actually broke out. But both sides built weapons—just in case.

The Cold War ended in 1991. Then the Minuteman sites began closing down.

The deactivated Minuteman missile is inside a glass silo at the Minuteman missile site.

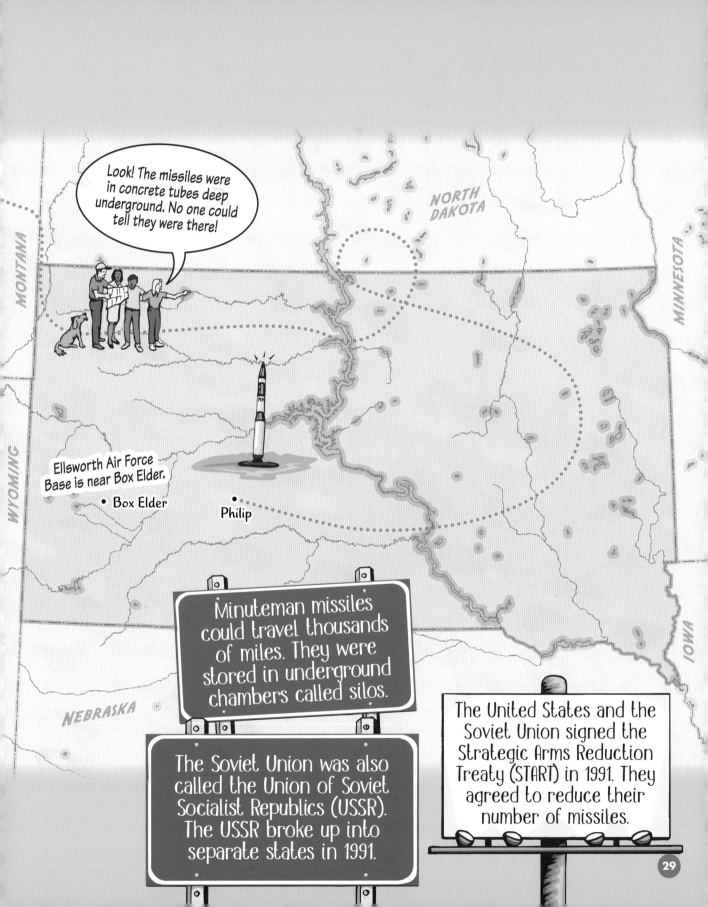

THE CORN PALACE IN MITCHELL

It looks like a big, colorful palace in Mitchell. Huge pictures cover its walls. But get up close. Those pictures are made of brightly colored corn!

This is the famous Corn Palace in Mitchell. Scenes of South Dakota life cover the walls. They're made with more than just corn. Many other grains and grasses are used, too.

South Dakotans are proud of their agriculture. That's why they built the Corn Palace!

Farms and ranches cover most of the state. Big ranches spread across western South Dakota. Most crops are grown in the east. Corn, soybeans, and wheat are the major crops.

Approximately 500,000 people visit the Corn Palace each year.

SHEARER'S COW CREEK RANCH IN WALL

Ride out on the range with the cowboys. Wear yourself out cleaning the horse stalls. Or just watch the cowboys work. You're at Shearer's Cow Creek Ranch in Wall!

This is a real cattle ranch. You can spend a whole vacation there. You can join the cowboys in their work. Or just sit back and watch.

South Dakota has thousands of cattle ranches. Beef cattle provide tons of meat. It's cut and packaged in meatpacking plants.

Meat processing is a big industry here. Some factories process milk, too. But computer equipment is the leading factory product.

Many farmers work on cattle ranches in South Dakota.

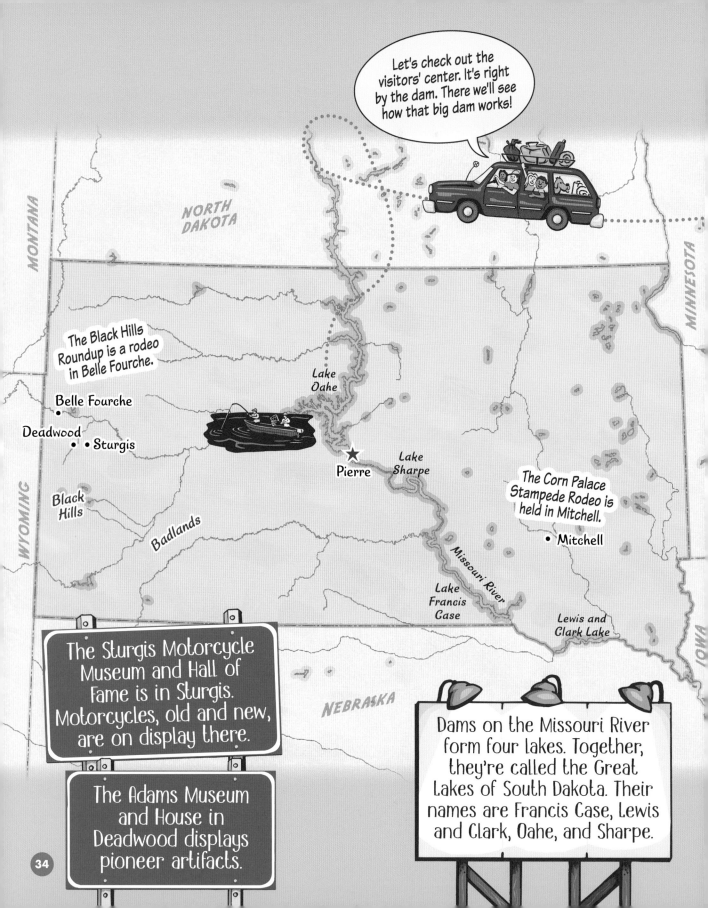

Let's check out the visitors' center. It's right by the dam. There we'll see how that big dam works!

MONTANA

NORTH DAKOTA

MINNESOTA

The Black Hills Roundup is a rodeo in Belle Fourche.

Lake Oahe

Belle Fourche

Deadwood • • Sturgis

Pierre

Lake Sharpe

The Corn Palace Stampede Rodeo is held in Mitchell.

• Mitchell

WYOMING

Black Hills

Badlands

Missouri River

Lake Francis Case

Lewis and Clark Lake

IOWA

NEBRASKA

The Sturgis Motorcycle Museum and Hall of Fame is in Sturgis. Motorcycles, old and new, are on display there.

The Adams Museum and House in Deadwood displays pioneer artifacts.

Dams on the Missouri River form four lakes. Together, they're called the Great Lakes of South Dakota. Their names are Francis Case, Lewis and Clark, Oahe, and Sharpe.

FUN AT LAKE OAHE

Jump in and make a big splash. Take a boat out and catch some fish. Or have a lakeside picnic under the trees. You're enjoying Lake Oahe!

This is South Dakota's biggest lake. It was created by Oahe Dam, near Pierre. That's a big dam on the Missouri River.

People have great fun on South Dakota's lakes. They enjoy the Black Hills and Badlands, too. Thousands of tourists visit the state every year. Some watch wildlife and take in the **scenery**. Others go to rodeos, powwows, or pioneer festivals. Historic sites are also popular. There's something for everyone in South Dakota!

Enjoy scenic views and fun outdoor activities at Lake Oahe.

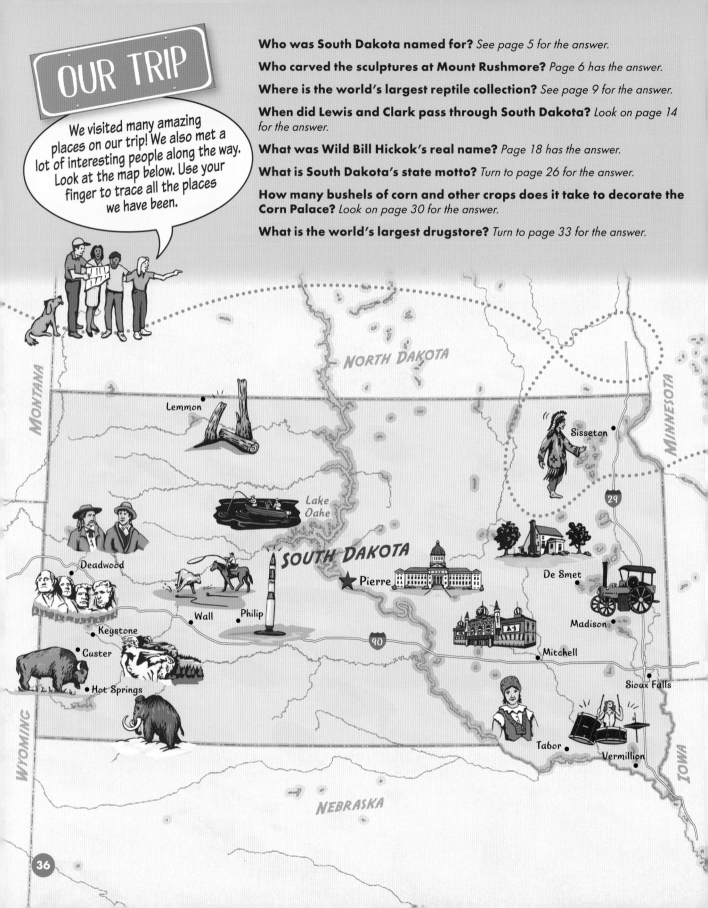

OUR TRIP

We visited many amazing places on our trip! We also met a lot of interesting people along the way. Look at the map below. Use your finger to trace all the places we have been.

Who was South Dakota named for? *See page 5 for the answer.*

Who carved the sculptures at Mount Rushmore? *Page 6 has the answer.*

Where is the world's largest reptile collection? *See page 9 for the answer.*

When did Lewis and Clark pass through South Dakota? *Look on page 14 for the answer.*

What was Wild Bill Hickok's real name? *Page 18 has the answer.*

What is South Dakota's state motto? *Turn to page 26 for the answer.*

How many bushels of corn and other crops does it take to decorate the Corn Palace? *Look on page 30 for the answer.*

What is the world's largest drugstore? *Turn to page 33 for the answer.*

MONTANA

NORTH DAKOTA

MINNESOTA

Lemmon

Sisseton

Lake Oahe

SOUTH DAKOTA

★ Pierre

De Smet

Deadwood

Madison

Wall

Philip

Keystone

Mitchell

Custer

Hot Springs

Sioux Falls

Tabor

Vermillion

WYOMING

NEBRASKA

IOWA

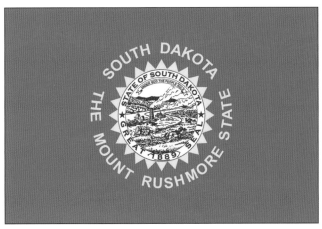

State flag

State seal

STATE SYMBOLS

State animal: Coyote

State bird: Chinese ring-necked pheasant

State dessert: Kuchen

State fish: Walleye

State flower: Pasque (May Day flower)

State fossil: *Triceratops*

State gemstone: Fairburn agate

State insect: Honeybee

State jewelry: Black Hills gold

State mineral: Rose quartz

State soil: Houdek soil

State tree: Black Hills spruce

STATE SONG

"HAIL, SOUTH DAKOTA"
Words and music by DeeCort Hammitt

Hail! South Dakota, A great state of the land,
Health, wealth and beauty, That's what makes her grand;
She has her Black Hills, And mines with gold so rare,
And with her scenery, No other state can compare.

Come where the sun shines, And where life's worth your while,
You won't be here long, 'Till you'll wear a smile.
No state's so healthy, and no folk quite so true,
To South Dakota. We welcome you.

Hail! South Dakota, The state we love the best,
Land of our fathers, Builders of the west;
Home of the Badlands, and Rushmore's ageless shrine,
Black Hills and prairies, Farmland and Sunshine.
Hills, farms and prairies, Blessed with bright Sunshine.

That was a great trip! We have traveled all over South Dakota. There are a few places that we didn't have time for, though. Next time, we plan to visit the National Music Museum in Vermillion. The museum has more than 10,000 musical instruments from countless cultures and historical periods. There are also live concerts and other activities.

FAMOUS PEOPLE

Anderson, Sparky (1934–2010), baseball manager

Barker, Bob (1923–), TV game show host

Bonnin, Gertrude (1876–1938), Dakota writer and activist

Brokaw, Tom (1940–), TV newscaster

Crazy Horse (ca. 1840–1877), Lakota chief

Ellis, Mark (1977–), baseball player

Goble, Paul (1933–), author

Hammon, Becky (1977–), basketball coach

Howe, Oscar (1915–1983), artist

Humphrey, Hubert H. (1911–1978), senator and vice president (1965–1969)

Jones, January (1978–), actor

Justus, Roy Braxton (1901–1983), political cartoonist

Lambert, Ward "Piggy" (1888–1958), basketball coach

Lawrence, Ernest (1901–1958), nuclear physicist

McGovern, George (1922–2012), politician

Means, Russell (1939–2012), Lakota activist

Miller, Mike (1980–), basketball player

Patrick, Jean L. S. (1961–), children's author

Red Cloud (1822–1909), Lakota chief

Sitting Bull (ca. 1831–1890), Dakota chief

Wilder, Laura Ingalls (1867–1957), author

Vinatieri, Adam (1972–), football player

WORDS TO KNOW

corrals (kuh-RALZ) holding pens for horses or other animals

fossils (FOSS-uhlz) the prints or remains of plants or animals left in stone

immigrants (IM-uh-gruhnts) people who move to another country

massacre (MASS-uh-ker) the violent killing of a large number of people

missile (MISS-uhl) a long, narrow weapon that travels a long distance

prairies (PRAIR-eez) grasslands

reservation (rez-ur-VAY-shuhn) land set aside for a special use, such as for Native Americans

scenery (SEE-nur-ee) a beautiful view of a nature area

threshing (THRESH-ing) separating grain or seeds from the stalks

traditional (truh-DISH-uhn-uhl) following long-held customs

TO LEARN MORE

IN THE LIBRARY

DiPrimio, Pete. *The Sioux of the Great Northern Plains.* Kennett Square, PA: Purple Toad, 2013.

Kelley, True. *Where Is Mount Rushmore?* New York, NY: Grosset & Dunlap, 2015.

Nelson, S. D. *Sitting Bull: Lakota Warrior and Defender of His People.* New York, NY: Abrams, 2015.

ON THE WEB
Visit our Web site for links about South Dakota:
childsworld.com/links

Note to Parents, Teachers, and Librarians: We routinely verify our Web links to make sure they are safe and active sites. So encourage your readers to check them out!

PLACES TO VISIT OR CONTACT
Travel South Dakota
travelsouthdakota.com
711 East Wells Avenue
Pierre, SD 57501
605/773-3301
For more information about traveling in South Dakota

South Dakota State Historical Society
history.sd.gov
900 Governors Drive
Pierre, SD 57501
605/773-3458
For more information about the history of South Dakota

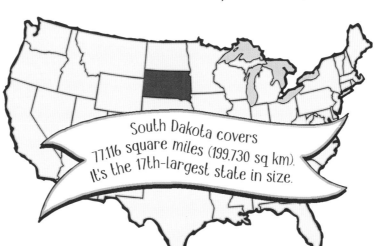

South Dakota covers 77,116 square miles (199,730 sq km). It's the 17th-largest state in size.

INDEX

Bye, Mount Rushmore State. We had a great time. We'll come back soon!